Namaste,
INDIA

by Corey Anderson

T0053989

CHERRY LAKE PUBLISHING · ANN ARBOR, MICHIGAN

Published in the United States of America by Cherry Lake Publishing
Ann Arbor, Michigan
www.cherrylakepublishing.com

Reading Adviser: Marla Conn MS, Ed., Literacy specialist, Read-Ability, Inc.

Book Design: Book Buddy Media

Library of Congress Cataloging-in-Publication Data has been filed and is available at catalog.loc.gov

Cherry Lake Publishing would like to acknowledge the work of The Partnership for 21st Century Learning.
Please visit www.p21.org for more information.

Printed in the United States of America

TABLE OF CONTENTS

CHAPTER 1

WELCOME TO INDIA!

With more than 1.2 billion people, India is home to about one-sixth of the world's population! At just about one-third the size of the United States, the country packs a lot of people into a relatively small area. India is a peninsula, which means it is almost completely surrounded by water. It is a land of mountain peaks, religious temples, crowded cities, and untouched beaches. India's unique culture is reflected in beautiful artwork, a booming film industry, colorful celebrations, and delicious foods found throughout the country.

The terrain of the town of Lamayuru is often compared to the moon due to its unusual rock formations and craters.

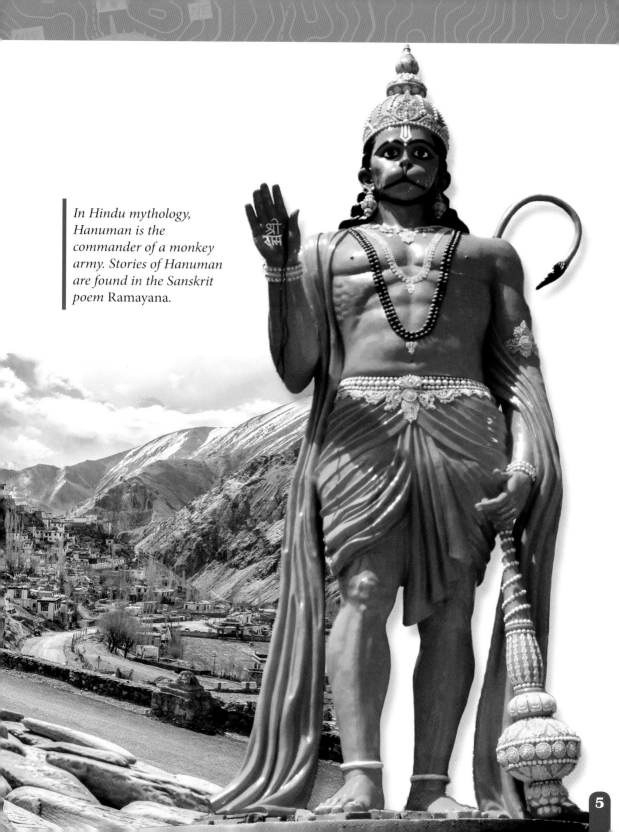

In Hindu mythology, Hanuman is the commander of a monkey army. Stories of Hanuman are found in the Sanskrit poem Ramayana.

ACTIVITY

Look at the map of India above. Notice the other countries that border it. Make note of the bodies of water that surround it. On a separate piece of paper, trace the outline of the country. See where New Delhi is? Mark that city with a star on your tracing. Also label the Himalayas. Now, label the Ganges River and the Krishna River. Do you see how the Ganges River cuts across the top of India?

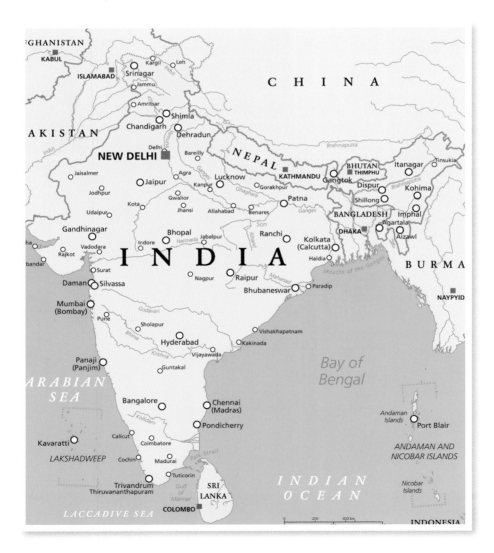

India's big cities are nearly as diverse as the country's geography. Many cities in India have more than 1 million residents. Mumbai is the largest city in India, with a population of more than 15 million people. It is well known for being a major port and industrial center. It is also the heart of the country's film business. Other cities, such as Chennai, draw sightseers to view a wide range of colorful, historic temples.

Bombay to Mumbai

Until 1995, when the name change became official, Mumbai was commonly known by its British name, Bombay. Today, Mumbai is a big, bustling city as varied as its residents. Within its boundaries exist a large tropical forest, sprawling **slums**, financial districts, and temples. It's a city that has also been challenged by pollution and transportation issues, making it difficult to navigate for many visitors.

More than 100 monks live at the Lamayuru Temple, where they learn and practice Buddhism.

The different regions of India all have different weather and landscapes. The Himalayas, northern plains, and the southern peninsula are three distinct regions in India. The Himalayas are a vast mountain range in northern India that stretches into other countries, including China. In the northern plains, farmland and some of India's biggest cities and attractions can be found.

The capital city of New Delhi and the beautiful monument the Taj Mahal are both located in the northern plains. The southern peninsula is home to a large plateau called the Deccan. It sits between two mountain ranges. It can be very arid, which means the area doesn't get a lot of rain.

The Thar Desert is also known as the Great Indian Desert. It helps to form a natural boundary between Pakistan and India.

India's Mountain Peaks

India is home to the third-highest mountain peak in the world, called Kangchenjunga. Located in the Himalayas, it is 28,169 feet (8,586 meters) tall and is located near the border of Nepal. It is also known as the "Five Treasuries of the Great Snow" because it has five distinct peaks.

India's climate can vary quite a bit, depending on the region of the country. Summer is very hot in most of India. Temperatures begin to increase in April, and the hottest time of the year is around June, when many areas are regularly more than 100 degrees Fahrenheit (38 degrees Celsius). Monsoon season starts around June as well, bringing heavy rains and sometimes destructive floods to areas located near rivers.

During monsoon season, it can be raining heavily one minute, and sunny just minutes later.

peacock

A recent study found that commuters spend 135 percent more time in their cars in Mumbai than in any other city in Asia.

In the northern part of the country, it can get very cold during the winters, bringing snow to the area. In the north, summers can be mild, while the rest of the country experiences heat waves.

India is the second-most populous country in the world, after China, and experiences many problems related to its high population. Unemployment, poverty, and traffic congestion are just a few problems that Indians face as the population continues to grow.

It is estimated that there are just over 2,000 Bengal tigers living in the wild in India today.

Given its diverse landscapes, it's no surprise that many different types of animals call India home. In fact, around 65,000 different animal species can be found there. Elephants, rhinoceroses, and water buffalos live in India, and it is the only country in the world where both tigers and lions roam free. Bengal tigers are typically found in Central or Northern India, and the Indian lion calls the state of Gujarat in western India home.

Indian Elephants

Indian elephants are **endangered** and on the brink of **extinction**. Smaller than African elephants, Indian elephants can still produce up to 220 pounds (100 kilograms) of poop every single day! Indian elephants are killed for their tusks, but only male elephants have tusks. This creates a population issue when more female than male elephants survive.

CHAPTER 2

BUSINESS AND GOVERNMENT IN INDIA

India's economy has been growing very quickly. It is projected to be one of the top economic powers in the world in the coming years. There will be up to 170 million people in India's labor force by 2020, with technology start-ups as a common area of industry.

At street markets in India, vendors sell a variety of wares, including colorful handmade shoes.

Despite the shift toward technology industries, most people in the Indian workforce still work in agriculture. The service industry is also important in India, providing jobs to many people. In India, many people work in customer service, taking phone calls to answer questions about computers, software, and other products for callers from around the world.

It is estimated that about 70 percent of India's farmwork is done by women.

To **export** products means to ship goods to other countries. India is the 17th-largest exporter in the world. More than 11 percent of India's exports are diamonds, making it the second-largest exporter of the beautiful gem in the world. **Petroleum** is another major export of India. Over half of India's exported goods are sold to other countries in Asia.

ECONOMY CHART

Here are the top exports from India by type:

Gems and precious metals: **$42.6 billion**

Mineral fuels, including oil: **$35.9 billion**

Machinery, including computers: **$16.7 billion**

Vehicles: **$16.2 billion**

Organic chemicals: **$13.6 billion**

Pharmaceuticals: **$12.9 billion**

Iron and steel: **$11.7 billion**

Clothing and accessories (not knitted or crocheted): **$9 billion**

Electrical machinery and equipment: **$8.8 billion**

Knitted or crocheted clothing and accessories: **$8.3 billion**

| 0 | 3% | 6% | 9% | 12% | 15% |

Instead of the dollar, the rupee is the currency used in India. It is abbreviated as ₹. The rupee is available in denominations of ₹1,000, ₹500, ₹100, ₹50, ₹20, ₹10, and ₹5 notes. One United States dollar is approximately the same value as 71 rupees.

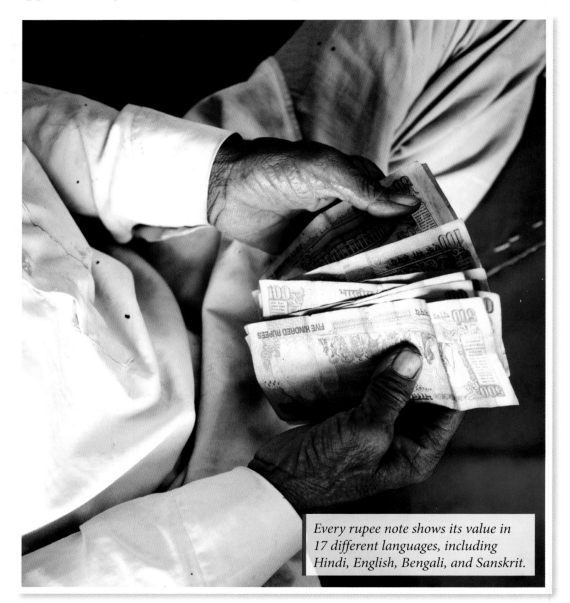

Every rupee note shows its value in 17 different languages, including Hindi, English, Bengali, and Sanskrit.

ACTIVITY

As of 2017, approximately 43 percent of India's people work in agriculture. Another 33 percent of the nation's labor force works in **manufacturing**. About 24 percent of India's people work in service industry jobs. Using this information, create a bar graph that shows these parts of India's economy. Ask a teacher or other adult for help if you need it. Label the horizontal axis of the bar graph "Type of industry." Label the vertical axis "Percentage of Indian workers." Don't forget to label each bar with the correct industry. Which bar will be longest? Which will be shortest?

India is one of the largest producers of tea in the world. The tea leaves are grown on sprawling plantations.

India has 7 national political parties and 24 state-recognized political parties.

India is the largest **democracy** in the world. A democracy is when citizens elect representatives to run the government. Great Britain controlled India for hundreds of years, but the Republic of India became independent in 1947.

Just like the United States, India has three branches of government—the executive, legislative, and judicial branches. In the executive branch, there is the president, the prime minister, and the Council of Ministers. The officials in the Council of Ministers are selected by the prime minister and appointed by the president. The Council of Ministers helps run different departments in the government.

Gandhi and Civil Rights

Mahatma Gandhi was a famous civil rights leader of India who helped lead the country to independence in the 1940s. He believed in nonviolent protests and peacefully worked for India's independence from the British empire. In addition, Gandhi also worked to secure other liberties and human rights for Indians. India officially gained its independence in 1947.

Indian Leadership

In India, the president generally does not exercise executive powers, but leads as more of a figurehead. It is similar to the role of a British king or queen. The Indian prime minister is actually the true head of government in India. The president does have some decision-making ability in special circumstances and makes important speeches as part of his or her role.

The Bharatiya Janata Party (BJP) is one of India's national political parties.

The Parliament of India sits in the legislative branch of the government. The Council of States and the House of the People make up Parliament. The representatives in the House of the People are elected by the citizens of India, and a select group from Parliament elects the president.

The Secretariat Building in New Delhi is where the Cabinet Secretariat administers India's government.

India's Female President

Pratibha Devisingh Patil served as the 12th president of India and held office for 5 years, from 2007 to 2012. She is the only woman to have served as president of the country. She worked as a lawyer before joining the Indian National Congress and eventually being elected as India's president.

The Rashtrapati Bhavan is the official home of the Indian president. It is located in New Delhi.

Just like in the United States, India's judicial branch upholds and enforces the laws of the land. The Supreme Court sits at the top of the judicial branch, with one chief justice and 30 other justices.

CHAPTER 3

MEET THE PEOPLE

India is home to over 1 billion people, and its citizens live in many types of environments. Many people live in close quarters, in small houses packed into crowded cities, such as New Delhi and Kolkata. In fact, there are more than 50 urban areas and cities throughout India with populations larger than 1 million people. But even today, over 60 percent of people that live in India reside in **rural** areas, like farms or villages in the countryside. These rural areas can be very simple, and people who live there might not have access to electricity or running water.

In rural areas of India, children often face poverty and poor living conditions.

The ethnicities of people who live in India vary a lot as well. The Dravidians of South India descend from the original inhabitants of the country, while the Indo-Aryans of the north are believed to have come to the land around 1800 BCE. There are many ethnic groups within the Indo-Aryan group, including Hindi, Marathi, and Punjabi. The Indo-Aryans have also produced many of the great **dynasties** of the country.

In India, red fabric often symbolizes prosperity or purity.

Many of the different ethnic groups of India have their own languages, but the central government uses Hindi as its official language, with English as a commonly used sub-language. The Constitution of India recognizes 22 different official languages spoken across the country. But there are many more dialects spoken as unofficial languages, with estimates of more than 1,000.

The colored powders used during the Holi celebration all have different symbolic meanings.

Hindu temples in India are often very colorful, or feature elaborate carvings and statues.

LANGUAGES

Hindi – 551 million speakers

English – 125 million speakers

Bengali – 91 million speakers

Telugu – 84 million speakers

Marathi – 84 million speakers

Tamil – 67 million speakers

Urdu – 59 million speakers

Kannada – 51 million speakers

Gujarati – 50 million speakers

Odia – 37 million speakers

With such a huge population, India runs the largest national school system on Earth. In fact, the country runs more than 700,000 schools in total. Many parents in India choose to put their children in private schools versus public schools. The first decade of a child's education, which starts at age 5, is **mandatory**. At age 14, schooling becomes optional. Many students continue on through secondary school. The school year in India typically runs from April through March, but that can vary, depending on the school.

The number of children who learn English at school in India has been increasing.

ACTIVITY

DRAW A HENNA HAND

In India, henna is the art of making beautiful temporary tattoos on hands and other parts of the body using dye from the henna plant.

Look at this picture of a hand painted with a henna design, and then draw your own henna pattern on a piece of paper.

1. Trace your hand on a piece of white paper.
2. Using a brown marker, draw your own henna design on the hand outline.
3. Consider drawing the following types of symbols on your hand, depending on what you want to communicate through your design:
   - Paisley symbolizes abundance.
   - Orange blossoms symbolize generosity.
   - The sun and moon symbolize deep love.

There are 28 different types of jewels set in the marble of the Taj Mahal.

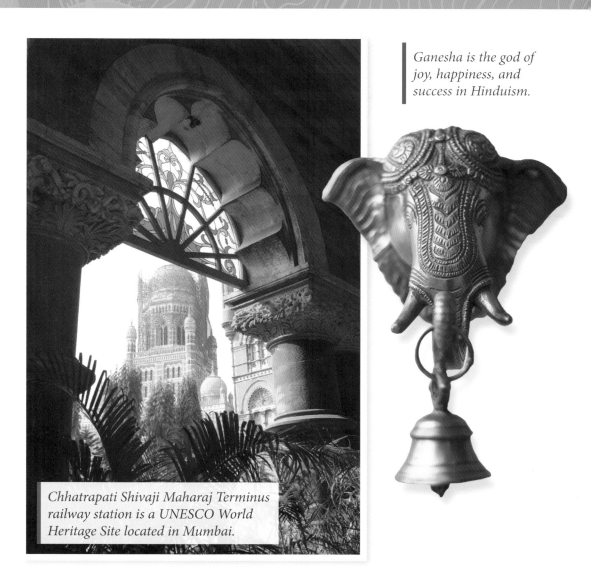

Chhatrapati Shivaji Maharaj Terminus railway station is a UNESCO World Heritage Site located in Mumbai.

Civilization in India began about 4,500 years ago, contributing to a very rich culture and many innovations. Architectural advances are seen in monuments like the Taj Mahal. The mathematical concept of zero was developed in India. Innovations in medicine, such as **Ayurveda**, were created in India. Today, Indian music, theater, and art is widely celebrated around the world.

The Popularity of Bollywood

Bollywood is the name given to the booming industry of Hindi-language movies in India. The name is a combination of "Bombay" and "Hollywood." Bollywood films are well known for being musicals, with song-and-dance numbers performed throughout the films. Many Bollywood movies are called "masala" films. Masala is a spice mixture, and "masala" movies are a mixture of elements such as comedy, thrills, and music.

CHAPTER 4

CELEBRATIONS

Many different religions are practiced in India. Hinduism is most common, with nearly 80 percent of India's citizens identifying as Hindus. More than 14 percent of people in India practice Islam, and they mostly live in the north or west parts of the country. Other religions that people follow in the country include Christianity, Sikhism, and Buddhism.

The Hindu Ganesh Chaturthi Festival celebrates the birth of the elephant-headed god Ganesh.

People light Diwali lamps to invite prosperity into their homes.

Colorful festivals are celebrated year round in India. For a stretch of 5 days sometime in October or November, Indians around the country celebrate Diwali, the grand festival of lights. During this festival, houses are decorated with clay lamps and candles, people wear new clothes, and treats are shared with family and friends. Diwali honors an important moment in Hindu history—the return of Lord Rama, along with his wife Sita and brother Lakshmana, after a 14-year exile.

Colored powders are thrown on the second day of Holi to celebrate the new beginnings of spring.

Holi is another beloved festival in India. Also known as the festival of colors, Holi is a vibrant holiday celebrated in February or March of every year. Holi signifies the victory of good, represented by Prince Prahlad, over evil, in the form of demoness Holika. On the eve of Holi, people sing and dance around bonfires. On Holi itself, people cover themselves and others in brightly colored dyes and sometimes toss balloons filled with colorful water.

MAJOR FESTIVALS

Holi – February or March
The festival of colors where people burn bonfires and toss brightly colored powders and water on each other.

Eid al-Fitr – June
A Muslim holiday that marks the end of Ramadan. It is a day for breaking the Ramadan fasts, when people enjoy great feasts and celebrations.

Raksha Bandhan – August
A festival to celebrate the bonds and love between brothers and sisters. Sisters often receive gifts from their brothers on this day.

Diwali – October or November
A holiday in which people exchange gifts and sweets, celebrating the story of the return of Lord Rama to the city of Ayodhya after a 14-year exile.

During Raksha Bandhan, gifts such as handmade items or money are given from brothers to sisters.

ACTIVITY

Perhaps you would like to read more books about India. If you do, get in the spirit by making a bookmark for your reading materials. Because India produces lovely gems, use colorful beads to remind yourself of the nation's beautiful jewelry.

MATERIALS:

- 20 inches (51 centimeters) of heavy cord
- beads with holes that are large enough for the cord to fit through
- ruler
- scissors

INSTRUCTIONS:

1. Sort your beads. Decide which ones you want to use and in what order.

2. Make a knot in the cord 3 inches (8 cm) from one end.

3. String beads through the opposite end of the cord. Work them along the cord until you reach the knot. Keep adding beads until you have created a 2-inch (5-cm) section of beads.

4. Make another knot, right next to the end of the beads you have added.

5. Use the ruler to measure 10 inches (25 cm) beyond that knot. Make another knot at that point. The cord between these two knots will remain empty. This part will go between the pages of the book you're reading.

6. String beads from this third knot for 2 inches (5 cm). Make a final knot at the end of the cord, right next to the beads you have just added.

7. Trim the ends of the cord using scissors. Leave 0.5 inches (1.3 cm) of cord on each end. Experiment with different kinds of cords and beads.

There are more than 30,000 sculptures covering the inside and outside of the Madurai Meenakshi temple.

The spiritual and physical practice of yoga began in India around 3,000 BCE. Although yoga began as a way to achieve harmony between the heart and soul, the physical benefits of yoga are also well known. Today, yoga is practiced by people all over the world and is thought to help treat many physical ailments and chronic pains.

Meditation, mantra chanting, and breathing techniques are all aspects of yoga taught in India.

CHAPTER 5

WHAT'S FOR DINNER?

The flavors of Indian **cuisine** are well loved not just in India, but also by people around the world. Many people seek out Indian restaurants to experience the country's unforgettable dishes. In India, the flavors and specialties vary by region, but they are generally divided into cuisine either from southern India or northern India.

Dishes served throughout the country use a wide variety of spices and herbs, such as garlic, ginger, turmeric, and cumin. Rice, chickpeas, and lentils are also highlighted in many dishes, but the particular flavors vary based on where in India the food is prepared.

Chutneys are a type of condiment commonly served with many meals in India.

Rava dosa *is a crepe-like treat often enjoyed with breakfast in India.*

Mumbai Street Food

Street food is very popular in Mumbai, and the foods reflect the diversity of the city's people. One of Mumbai's most popular street foods is *vada pav*, which is like a burger, but the patty is made of a fried mashed potato mixture. It's also common to find chai being sold on the streets of Mumbai. Chai is a spicy type of tea, which is served up with warm milk and extra spices, for an especially soothing and enjoyable treat.

Every region in India has its own particular cooking styles and popular dishes. Although most food in India is vegetarian, there are dishes that feature ingredients like fish, goat, chicken, and other meats. In South Indian cuisine, coconut oil or coconut meat is commonly used, providing a unique flavor in many foods.

Cardamom, cumin, coriander, and turmeric are spices commonly found in Indian foods.

Dadpe pohe *is a snack made from beaten rice and spices.*

The cuisine in the north is influenced by the cooking styles of central Asia. Buttery curries, *ghee*, kebabs, and *samosas* are trademarks of the food in the north. *Samosas* are small pockets of pastry stuffed with savory filling, then deep-fried until golden. Since wheat grows well in the region, breads like *roti* and *tandoori* are popular there as well.

Indian Desserts

Many people in India have a sweet tooth, leading to the creation of delicious dessert creations served throughout the country. *Kheer* is a milk pudding that is served up with spices like saffron and cardamom, along with dried fruits and nuts. *Kaju barfi* is another beloved sweet treat. It looks like a yellow fudge, but it is made from cashews. It is a more expensive treat to find in the country and is often given out as a gift for special occasions.

In India, farmers sometimes walk long distances to carry supplies between locations.

RECIPE

There are many different Indian foods to try. Here is an easy recipe to start with. Ask an adult to help, especially with any chopping or when using appliances.

MANGO LASSI

INGREDIENTS

- 1 cup (235 milliliters) of plain yogurt
- 1/4 cup (60 ml) of milk
- 1 cup (165 grams) of chopped mangoes
- 1/2 cup (35 g) of ice
- 4 teaspoons (16 g) of sugar
- ground cardamom

INSTRUCTIONS

1. Wash and peel the mangoes. Carefully chop the fruit into small pieces. Remove the pit.

2. Place the yogurt, milk, mango, ice, and sugar in a blender. Blend for 2 minutes, or until smooth.

3. Pour into glasses and sprinkle cardamom on top. Enjoy!

The lassi *can be kept refrigerated for 24 hours. Experiment with other fruits.*

Thali *is a round dish used to serve up many different types of foods in India.*

In India, people often eat food with their fingers instead of using utensils. It is believed that eating with your hands helps you to better appreciate the food. Also, there are not first or second courses in India. Instead, food is served all at once and is often served family-style. That means the dishes are placed at the center of the table so each guest can serve themselves, instead of being served one dish at their place setting.

In India, it is common to eat with the right hand, but not the left.

GLOSSARY

cuisine *(kwi-ZEEN)* a style or way of cooking or presenting food

democracy *(dem-AHK-ruh-see)* a political system in which the people elect leaders to represent them in government

endangered *(in-DAYN-juhrd)* when a type of plant or animal is at risk of dying out

export *(EK-sport)* to sell and ship to another country

extinction *(eks-TINGK-shuhn)* no longer living

mandatory *(MAN-duh-tor-ee)* required

manufacturing *(man-yuh-FAK-chuh-ring)* the making of products, often with the use of equipment

petroleum *(puh-TROH-lee-uhm)* oil that is taken from the earth and used to make gasoline and other products

rural *(RUR-uhl)* having to do with the country or farming

slums *(SLUHMZ)* very poor, crowded, and rundown housing areas in a city

FOR MORE INFORMATION

BOOKS

Hoffman, Susannah. *Yoga for Kids.* New York: DK Publishing, 2018.

Nardo, Don. *Understanding Hinduism.* San Diego, CA: ReferencePoint Press, 2019.

Wood, Alix. *Uncovering the Culture of Ancient India.* New York: Rosen Publishing Group, Inc., 2016.

WEB SITES

Digital Dialects—Hindi Language Games
http://www.digitaldialects.com/Hindi.htm
Learn and practice Hindi words and phrases with these interactive games.

National Geographic Kids—India
https://kids.nationalgeographic.com/explore/countries/india/
Read more about the history, government, and culture of India.

Kids World Travel Guide
https://www.kids-world-travel-guide.com/india-for-kids.html
Learn more about the geography, attractions, animals, and people of India.

INDEX

ABOUT THE AUTHOR

Corey Anderson is a writer and editor based in the Los Angeles area. When not typing away at a computer, Corey enjoys exploring Southern California with her two sons and husband, and participating in running races and other athletic pursuits.